FALL OF CONSTANTINE'S CHRISTIAN EMPIRE

A Renewed Call to Transformation

By

GARY R UREMOVICH, PHD

Your book has been assigned a free KDP ISBN:
ISBN: 9798369696941
Imprint: Independently published

DEDICATION

I am indebted to my beloved wife, Viveca Yoshikawa. We are newlyweds (2 years at the publication of this book). She encouraged and supported me during my seminary education and with the writing of this book. She spent hours editing my dissertation and this book. I don't know if she knew what she was getting into when I proposed to her. I am so blessed that she has such a knowledge of linguistics. She is fluent in so many languages! Her editorial skills are amazing, especially since English is her second language (she is Swedish). Let me be clear, any errors in syntax, grammar, or spelling are my fault! I had the habit of changing the manuscript after she did her editing!

ACKNOWLEDGMENT

I am thankful beyond measure for my Pastor, Justin LaRosa, who has shown me what it means to share the love of Christ with the homeless and the outsider. His courage to welcome the outcast and marginalized has brought a new sense of the Gospel message to me. Instead of preaching at pews, we meet in small groups around tables with face-to-face interaction. During these times of sharing, we have unscripted discussions of Scripture. This has been a formative experience in my Christian growth. This book is just one small product of that experience.

AUTHOR'S BIO.

Gary is a retired Lt Colonel (USAF) with 26 years of service, a Physician Assistant (Emeritus) with 42 years of clinical practice, a medical and faith-based educator, and a seminary graduate. He has previously served as the Director of Protestant Religious education at the USAF Wright Patterson AFB Chapel. He specializes in facilitating small groups. He is authoring a series of books that may be used in various group settings. For more information contact Growth Group Publishing by emailing GrowthGroupPublishing@gmail.com.

TABLE OF CONTENTS

FOREWORD

Let me be very clear. I love Jesus and the Church! Within its ministries, I have found grace, peace, encouragement, purpose, and (most importantly) salvation and unconditional love. I cannot imagine a life without Jesus at its center. Even so, as I look at our history over the last 2,000 years, I am troubled. How could faith in the "Prince of Peace" have been instrumental in so much violence, hatred, and persecution?

I have been inspired by the title of a book written about Constantine's appropriation of the Christian faith as an 'Empire' which was written by a professor of Ancient Medieval History and Latin (Charles Matson Odahl) in 2004. The book was simply entitled "Constantine and the Christian Empire." I am convinced that the Christian faith was never meant to become an 'empire' – it was intended to be (and continues to be) a revolution of love, self-sacrifice, and personal transformation.

This will not be some dry history book. I want the reader to be motivated to explore these important issues more thoroughly on their own. This is not an academic or historical book like the 'Rise and Fall of the Roman Empire.' I do hope that this short book will cause you to think and do your own research into our history as a people of faith. Perhaps you will see how we have fallen short of the Christian faith in place of Constantine's vision of a religious Empire.

This book is the result of my personal journey of faith. I am shocked by how far our faith has wandered from Christ. Our religion is something that Jesus would not recognize or endorse. Personally, I have had many wonderful experiences in the church. But I also know that the church has injured many over the last 2,000 years. This book needs to be written. I love Jesus and His people too much to stay quiet any longer.

Yes, I am painfully troubled by the organized religion that bears His name. Are you? How can we, who call ourselves Christians, be so much different than Jesus? How can we be so self-righteous and condescending to so many? We are told that, here in the US, Christianity will no longer be the dominant religion within a couple of decades. We appear to be in the last throes of vanishing from the earth as an empty and meaningless religion. Christianity is failing. At one time we were pre-eminent among the world's religions. After all, who wouldn't want to be associated with a Savior who loves everyone unconditionally? If only we had left it at that – boundless, unconditional, transformative love for everyone. I believe we have lost that impact of love in the world!

Today, we have inherited a Christianity that desires to be culturally powerful in all its denominational brands. The problem is that both the East and West versions of our religion are based on a power protocol developed by Constantine himself. From the earliest years of our faith until today, Christianity has been a political, military, and ruthless social power. Sadly, this is devoid of the elements of Christ's image of a new Creation based on His Kingdom and personal transformation. As He told Pilate, His kingdom was not of this World (see John 18:36-37). It appears that we have rejected the Kingdom of Christ for the Kingdom of Man. We need a renewed vision of Christ's Kingdom. My goal in writing this book is to ask the hard questions and to start a dialogue – it is merely a beginning.

I expect that what I have to say will engender controversy and pushback. I hope that happens! Each chapter will include questions at the conclusion to encourage conversation in small groups. I am convinced that questions are always more important than answers. Our religion has been exceptional in providing answers to questions that nobody is asking. Good and relevant questions keep us in dialogue while neat and tidy platitudes end conversations. Our journey, as a people of faith, is too important for easy and meaningless cliches.

We need to revise our vision of our faith from one of power, superiority, and dominance to one of love and self-sacrifice. It is an imperative that must not be ignored.

CHAPTER 1: PRE-CONSTANTINE CHRISTIANS: A COUNTERCULTURAL FAITH

I used to think how wonderful it was that Emperor Constantine 'saved' the Christian faith through his conversion. I thought it remarkable that faith in a crucified carpenter from a little town in Israel could become the victor over the Roman Empire. Faith in Christ was now the official state religion! However, while doing research for this book, I discovered that it is far more complicated than that!

There were sporadic waves of persecution of Christians during the first three hundred years under Emperors Nero, Diocletian, Domitian, and Vespasian. Despite this, Christians were thriving and making a truly countercultural difference in the Roman Empire. An interesting point is the demographics of the Roman Empire around AD 300. Despite waves of persecution, Christianity had grown steadily in both numbers and social influence.

Christians were incredibly faithful and resilient people. Prior to this, Roman religion was something you were born into. Now, you could, by faith, become a Christian without regard to nationality, privilege, or position. These Christians were also shockingly fearless in their faith. They had no fear of death or aversion to pain. They were firm in their profession of faith and willingly suffered martyrdom. The extent of their persecution and torture was sickening. Even the pagans around them sought to hide them from the authorities. John Firth (1904) writes

> "...that he [Athanasius) often heard survivors of the persecution say that many pagans risked the loss of their goods and the chance of imprisonment in order to hide Christians from the officers of the law. There

> is no question of exaggeration. The most horrible tortures were invented; the most barbarous and degrading punishments were devised. The victim who was simply ordered to be decapitated or drowned was highly favored. In a very large number of cases, death was delayed as long as possible. The sufferer, after being tortured on the rack, or having eyes or tongue torn out, or foot or hand struck off, was taken back to prison to recover for a second examination (p. 13)"

Christians served in all aspects of the Roman Empire including the royal court, the military, and civil society. Out of a total population of 60 million in the Roman Empire, 3 million were Christians and Jews numbering about 11 million (Denova, Rebecca 2021). Christians were found in all the Empire. In some regions, Christianity was the dominant religion: "…there were regions in the Empire in which [Christianity] was not far from representing the half, or even the majority, of the population. This was the case, for instance, in Asia Minor. In northern Syria, in Egypt, and in Africa, the Christians were also very numerous" (Duchesne, 2018, p. 5).

These Christians had many diverse beliefs and various theological understandings of the faith. Even so, the unity they experienced by following Jesus was amazing. There was no unifying doctrine, just a relationship with the 'Unifier' who said He would draw all people to Himself (see John 12:32). These Christians were formidable in their loyalty to Jesus and willingness to die for their faith. They were considered people of integrity and good character. Because of these qualities, they often rose to positions of responsibility throughout the government, trades, and military. They demonstrated their strength of character by being steadfast on moral issues.

Within the Roman Empire, it was the Christians who stood out and demonstrated profound courage, and unfailing faith. It seemed that all who professed Christ were fearless in the face of torture and even a terrible death. This was true of young children, parents, and the elderly. While many Christians were pacifists, there were also large numbers of Christians in the Roman military as well as in the Empire's elite.

These early believers were valiant and fiercely counter-cultural. They refused to back down from a ruthless Empire when it came to their faith. Firth (1904) again notes:

> "In the presence of such splendid fidelity and such unswerving faith, which made even the weakest strong and able to endure, one sees why the eventual triumph of the Church was certain and assured (p. 17)."

Despite such brutal treatment, Christians were winning the culture war. They were standing up and being counted despite being challenged to recant their faith. They weren't just withstanding persecution; they were increasing in numbers of faithful followers. They were in every station of life and were demonstrating courage, integrity, and moral fiber. Imperial evil was being confronted and defeated with bold and willing martyrdom. This was the world's first taste of nonviolent resistance and Christians were winning. The love of Christ was overturning the world with passionate believers.

Discussion:

1. Why do you think Christianity was so popular despite intense persecution?
2. Why did not having a cohesive doctrine or dogma make little difference in the rapid growth of Christianity?
3. Professing Christians were given high positions in various roles because of integrity and faithfulness. Does being a Christian have the same significance today? Why or why not?
4. We have differing doctrines in various Christian denominations today. How does that seem to affect us differently than it did the early Church?

CHAPTER 2: CONSTANTINE'S CONVERSION

Emperor Constantine had a vision prior to a battle with a contender for the throne of the Roman Empire, Maxentius. He was outnumbered 2-1 and it appeared he would be defeated unless a miracle happened. Constantine was also in trouble in numerous other areas such as taxes, conflicts, wars, unrest within the Empire, and family feuds (Constantine the Great, Wikipedia). History tells us that Constantine was preparing for a battle with Maxentius, who had twice as many soldiers as he. The night before the battle (Milvian Bridge, 28 October AD 312), "Constantine…saw with his own eyes the trophy of a cross of light in the heavens, above the sun, and bearing the inscription, *In Hoc Signo Vinces*" ["In this sign, thou shalt conquer"]." He had his soldiers place the superimposed chi and rho (XP) symbols on their shields to represent the first two Greek letters of Christ. The following day each soldier had the letters on their shields. As Christians, we seem to accept this vision and vindicate Constantine's military use of our faith.

Was this a conversion? There was no sense of needing a Savior for his soul. He needed a god to defeat his enemies. It's interesting that Emperor Constantine never became a Christian (by baptism) until his deathbed. We tend to think that his vision in the sky was evidence of his conversion. There are problems with that assertion! Suppose you have a friend who sees clouds in the shape of Jesus with the words "kill all unbelievers." What would you say? Would you recommend that your friend follow through on this vision? Of course not! You would probably call the authorities and ensure that your friend seeks medical help – immediately.

I am trying to make an important point. Many people have dreams or visions that make them wonder if God is communicating with them. The best way for us to know if God is sending a message is to see if this 'vision' conforms to God's written word. Jesus would never have His name and symbol used for killing anyone – even His enemies. Furthermore, these were only political enemies of Constantine. Obviously, this does not reflect the values of the Christian God Who loves all people.

Let us remember that emperor Constantine was a pagan and actively practiced his religion. He was a worshiper of the Roman sun god (Invictus Sol— 'Unconquered Sun') which he had printed on his coins with his own image. For him, there was only one God who was the 'sun god.' In other words, he was a pagan monotheist. Researchers find that it is probable that he had a couple of visions. This first vision occurred two years prior to the vision he had at the battle of Milvian Bridge. This initial vision was of the sun god. Some believe that there were not two visions but just one which has been historically conflated. This vision may have been a natural phenomenon as described online by the British historian A.H.M. Jones (2019). The "vision" was a "halo" — the Greek word *halos* means "solar disk" in English. This occurs due to the refraction of light in a cloud containing ice crystals. This phenomenon causes the sun to refract into the shape of a cross.

Possible "Solar Halo" that might have been seen by Emperor Constantine. A natural phenomenon caused by ice crystals causing a flaring of the sun.

Constantine was an incredible military commander and social engineer. Some question whether he had a valid mystical experience. His vision might have been a natural phenomenon. It almost seems too convenient to be true. Here is how one historian explores this issue. I also tend to be more cynical since historically Rome's and Constantine's hold on regional, political, and military power was crumbling.

> "… Others have a more cynical view of Constantine's motives and have suggested that he simply tapped into what he already knew was a powerful movement for his own political benefit. At any rate, Constantine was indeed a successful military commander and went on to become a successful imperial ruler (History, Hourly, 2021, p. 39)."

This becomes even more suspect in the writings of the historian, Eusebius. It appears that it was a public relations effort.

> "The Life of Constantine was not the first volume of contemporary history published by Eusebius. He had already written a History of the Church, which he issued to the world in AD 326. What, then, had the author to say in that year about this marvelous vision? Nothing. There is not a word about the flaming cross or the coming of Christ to Constantine in a dream, or the fashioning of the Labarum. All Eusebius says, in his [Treatise on Constantine's] History, of the conversion of Constantine, is that the Emperor "piously called to his aid the God of Heaven and his son Jesus Christ" It is a strange silence. If the heavenly cross had been seen by the whole army; if the current version of the story had been the same in 326 as it was in 337, it is at least difficult to understand why Eusebius omitted all mention of an event that must have been the talk of the whole Roman world and must have made the heart of every Christian exult (Firth, 1904, p. 45)."

Constantine won the battle and is said to have credited his victory to Jesus of Nazareth. We are told that, because of this miraculous victory, he wanted the Roman Empire to be united under the banner of Jesus. Wow! The persecuted Church was now going to be officially recognized and honored. What a triumph over Satan! I have often thought that this was a wonderful movement of the Spirit. Finally, Jesus wins. The problem was that it might have been a political stunt to bring more power to the Roman Empire.

It appears that Constantine wanted a more robust and powerful religion that would unite the Empire. Some believe that his conversion was more of a political and military move rather than the product of a spiritual conviction. There was no spiritual crisis that compelled Constantine to embrace Christ. He was a devoted follower of the sun god and continued to produce his coins with the emblem of the sun god for another 10 years or until AD 323 (Kee, 1982, p. 20).

Is it surprising that the origin of organized Christianity was founded on the battlefield? What would Jesus have said about that? How dare we weaponize our faith in pursuit of a victorious war? We see many examples in history of how a weaponized Christianity has led to much death and destruction (8 major Crusade campaigns, Protestant/Catholic wars, many other religious wars, sectarian hatred, and racial/gender bigotry). While the Roman Empire met its downfall 2,000 years ago, we now see that our weaponized religion is losing its attraction and adherents.

The problem was (and continues to be) that the origin of our organized religion was the product of a military and political agenda. As a young Christian, I used to enjoy singing the chorus "Onward Christian Soldiers" with its refrain to fight the enemy with the catchy phrase 'marching as to war.' We will explore other aspects of our religion that encourage violence. This violence is verbal, physical, systematic, and entrenched in religious jargon. This must change. Some theologians talk about the 'Constantine shift' (Wikipedia) where Christianity changed from being a persecuted religion to a persecuting one.

Discussion:

1. What were your expectations as you started to read this book?
2. How do you react to the violent origin of the 'official' Christian religion?
3. What reaction do you think Jesus would have to Emperor Constantine?
4. How are we a persecuting religion? Is that statement going too far?
5. Do you have other examples of how our religion has been weaponized?

Crusaders on the advance.

CHAPTER 3: THE ROMAN EMPIRE VERSUS THE KINGDOM OF GOD

Constantine never understood the message of Jesus. His 'conversion' was never a realization of his weakness and sin. Instead, it was a means to an end, to conquer his foes. He remained a pagan for his entire life. He saw the power and devotion that Jesus had over His adherents. They were willing to be tortured and die in the name of Jesus. In his magical thinking, Constantine saw an image that he thought could revolutionize his soldiers and bring fear into the hearts of his foes. The One Who said "love your enemies" would never have approved of using His name to kill in battle.

As noted in the last chapter, I mentioned John 18: 36-37 where Jesus told Pilate that his followers would not fight because His kingdom is not of this realm. He still tells us the same thing today, let's stop fighting! After all, the Bible says that whoever hates his brother is a murderer (1 John 3:15). Jesus took a step further, if you're angry with your brother without a cause you are in danger of judgment (Matthew 5:21).

You might say that it doesn't matter how Constantine embraced Christianity. After all, it's ancient history. Unfortunately, we continue to see and use our faith in terms of power over others. How many wars have been waged over our faith? Perhaps we no longer have conflicts on the battlefield. But we still have religious intolerance, racism, sexism, and many other forms of prejudice and hatred; we continue to fight. Someone has astutely said, that the most segregated time of the week is on Sunday, when Christians meet in their separate churches.

Perhaps one of the clearest (if not disarming) teachings on the Kingdom of God by Jesus is demonstrated by the Sermon on the Mount (Matthew 5). In His sermon, we see society's values turned upside down. This is a revolutionary vision. Not in the political or military sense, but in how we as humans view life! It is not based on power, prestige, or possessions. Living within the Kingdom of God is based on love and sacrifice. These are spiritual values that rulers such as Constantine (or Pilate) would never embrace or even understand.

Roman Soldiers in Battle. These are not the Christian missionaries we normally think of!

Listen to some of the themes from Matthew 5 and see if any of these 'warriors' could be found on Emperor Constantine's battlefield. The poor in spirit, those who mourn, the meek, those who thirst for righteousness, the merciful, the peacemakers, the persecuted, and those who are insulted. These are not combatants of an Emperor. Unfortunately, these spiritual principles do not reflect our society's values (nor of the typical Christians) either.

Jesus goes on in that same chapter calling us the light of the world and the salt of the earth. Qualities that bring unity, preservation, community, warmth, and peace. This was not the sort of kingdom that would include warfare and killing. Jesus told His disciples that the Kingdom of God was already present (Luke 10:9). This kingdom is within the hearts of those who follow Jesus – not into combat, but into a life of sacrificial love. We are told to seek the Kingdom first (Matthew 6:33) instead of all the earthly 'things' we think we need.

I find notable that the Christian Church, however flawed, is still here while the Roman Empire has gone the way of antiquity. Even so, we still have the remnants of Constantine's view of a religious and violent empire. We must remove the 'Empire' attitude within our religion. The Christian faith has survived over 2,000 years because of its profound and beautiful connection of the divine with humanity. It is an eternal message of love and redemption.

Discussion:

1. Do we still have an 'empire' attitude within our religion? What does this mean?
2. How do we still fight and try to injure our adversaries?
3. How do Christians typically relate to adherents of another faith? How would Jesus?
4. Review the Sermon on the Mount (Matthew 5: 1-15). How do these principles reflect the Kingdom of God?
5. What do you think is preventing us from becoming the salt of the earth and the light of the world?

Constantine's 'Christian' Army.

CHAPTER 4: CHRISTIANITY BEFORE CONSTANTINE

We are so naïve about early church history from almost 2,000 years ago. We do not know how they practiced and defended their faith in such a hostile culture. The Jewish culture considered them heretics, while the pagan Romans considered them atheists. To the Romans, an atheist was anyone who either had no god or had a god who could not be seen. Rome had altars and statues of many gods. They even worshipped Caesar as an emperor god. Christians were, therefore, atheists because they worshiped an invisible non-physical god. In addition, Romans valued strength, power, and prestige. It made no sense that Christians would worship a hidden god who died as a scorned criminal, was poor, homeless, meek, and helpless.

Christians were persecuted on and off. Much of the post-apostolic area was free from violent persecution. However, there were times of intense persecution, with many Christians dying as martyrs. Christians were unique and stood out from the Romans and the Jews. They lived lives that were based on a solid faith demonstrated by Christian values, such as sharing with the poor, not lying, not cheating, and loving even your enemies. They obeyed Roman laws if they were not asked to deny the Lordship of Jesus or offer worship to an idol. That irked some Roman authorities and led to confrontations.

Research has discovered many writings during the pre-Nicene period by theologians and early church leaders. These authors were prolific and shared their works and the local churches. One such writing was the Didache (also known as The Teaching of the Twelve Apostles). It was an early Christian manual written sometime between the first and second centuries. In effect, it reflected the teachings of Christianity as a manual of behavior (Owles, R., 2014).

In this manual, early converts were taught about the way of life (living a life honoring Christ), and the way of death (not following Christ), baptism, how to recognize true prophets, and how to celebrate the Eucharist, to name a few. Many things were discussed, such as abortion, infanticide, fasting, prayer, lying, giving to the poor, doing right, and lovingly treating others. All Christians were expected to follow these teachings.

Tertullian was a Latin scholar from Tunis in Africa during the second century AD (155-220). He wrote volumes in Latin which could be understood by the Romans. He would even write to the Emperor and the Senate, defending Christians against their faulty understanding of the faith. He was a prolific writer, converted from paganism, and was probably trained as a lawyer. He is often referred to as the first theologian of the Western Church (Roman). Here is one of his statements. It is a long but fascinating view of the early church. He initially refutes some false accusations against Christians and then beautifully describes their practice in paragraph 39 of his defense (Christian History Institute, #104).

> "Having refuted the charges laid against us, let me now show what we really are. We are a body knit together by one faith, one discipline and one hope. We meet together as a congregation, uniting together to offer prayer to God. We pray for the emperors and all in authority, for the welfare of the world, for peace and for the delay of the final end. We read our holy scriptures to nourish our faith, hope, steadfastness and good habits. We hear exhortations and rebukes. We take such judging very seriously – as befits those who believe they are in the sight of God – especially seriously when anyone sins so grievously we have to cut them off from our prayer, our congregation and all sacred things. Our elders preside over us, obtaining that honor not by money, but by their established character. There is no buying and selling in the things of God. Though we have a fund, but not because people can buy religion. Once a month, anyone who wants to makes a small donation – but only he who

> is able and willing; there is no compulsion. It is not spent on feasts, but to support and bury poor people, to provide for orphans, the elderly old persons, victims of shipwreck and those in prison for their faith."

This is only one example of the type of work available before Constantine. We had many such Apostolic Fathers who were equally talented in writing about the faith based on contact with the Apostles. Clement of Rome (possibly mentioned by Paul in Philippians 4:3) was a disciple of Paul and Peter and echoed their apostolic teachings. Polycarp, Ignatius, and Papias were all associates of the Apostle John. Other authors include Justin Martyr, Ignatius of Antioch, and a mystical epistle called 'Shepherd of Hermes.' In other words, Christians were actively writing about their faith and defending it against Roman antipathy. There is a reference available on Kindle (for free at the time I accessed it), which can give you an idea of the quality and volume of material written during this time (Roberts, A and Donaldson, J., 2014). I could reference many of these authors. However, I could never provide the depth of discussion they can provide in their literary works!

My reason for discussing the pre-Nicene era is that Christians were actively (but non-violently) expressing, defending their faith, and living out their faith publicly. I am sure Constantine was aware of this group's intellectual, spiritual, and moral vigor. I think that had more of an impact on his seeing the strength in this religious sect. This was also when all Christians knew there could be a high price for living out their faith. The Romans were amazed at their courage. Early Christians' faith was defined by how faithfully they lived and not by what beliefs they assented to. In a pagan society, having different brands (denominations) of the faith did not matter. It was spiritual unity in the way of life based on a faithful love of the Savior.

I think our society is becoming more like pagan Rome. Fewer people profess a religious affiliation. When asked about religious affiliation, many people say 'none.' Our Western culture reflects the values of pagan Rome – power, position, and possessions are becoming our gods. It is all about materialism. The impact of the pre-Nicene Christians was their ability to live a life honoring God that could not be ignored. In today's culture, we need that! We need to live a life that reflects our faith rather than just having rhetoric about what we believe and how our creed is different from others. Jesus said: 'by this shall all men know that you are my disciples, that you love one another" (John 13:35). It was true in pagan Rome, and it is still true today.

Discussion:

1. Why were Christians in pagan Rome called atheists? What confused the Roman Empire about the faith of Christians?
2. For early Christians, what was more important – 'what' they believed or how they lived? What do you think is most essential for us today? What difference does it make?
3. Do you see evidence that we are more like pagan Rome with materialistic idols (power, position, and possessions)?
4. If we had the kind of persecution of our faith in Jesus as first-century Christians, would we stand up and (non-violently) defend the faith? How?
5. Tertullian said (in his defense of Christianity) that 'we were one body knit together.' Is that still true today? Why or why not?

CHAPTER 5: THE PAGANIZATION OF CHRISTIANITY

The Church sold its moral and spiritual standing to Constantine. According to Britannica, a Faustian bargain is "a pact whereby a person trades something of supreme moral or spiritual importance, such as personal values or the soul, for some worldly or material benefit, such as knowledge, power, or riches." This is what happened in AD 312 when Constantine 'embraced' Christianity.

Constantine was transforming the faith of Christians into a more imperialistic form that would change society and the Christian faith. Alistair Kee (1982):

> "...in gathering up lines of thought often already present in the church and developing them in a certain way, they combine to affect something which had never been accomplished here thereto, the replacement of the norms of Christ and the early church by the norms of the imperial ideology. Why it has been previously thought that Constantine was a Christian is not because what he believed was Christian, but because what he believed came to be called Christian. And this represents the 'triumph of ideology.' (p. 4)"

I question why the Christian faith leaders gave in so quickly to Constantine's overtures. Perhaps you think it was all about self-preservation. As noted previously, the Christian faith was growing and flourishing without help from the Roman Empire. Constantine was an expert at co-opting religious concepts and mingling them with his pagan background.

Please stick with me on this! Here is a list of all the paganized areas of our faith inculcated by Constantine and his followers. My purpose is not to disturb your faith but to reinforce the faith given to us! My goal is to have you do your research and check each of these areas for yourself. I could spend much time on each one of these aspects of our paganized faith.

The Cross. The cross on which Christ was crucified did not have a crossbar. The Greek word for the cross was "Stauros," which meant a pole (Stauros, Wikipedia) without any crossbar. Often referred to as the tree. The cross in our faith is found in many other religions. Initially, the two-beam cross symbolized the god Tammuz as the Mystic Tau (Davis, 2006, p. 43). I always thought how odd it was to have the implementation of Christ's death (the cross) represent our faith. As a symbol of ancient religions, this might have made pagans embrace our faith more efficiently since there was an emblem they recognized. Today, it is a common symbol for jewelry and household decorations and is found in almost all churches.

The Halo. This was originally a symbol of the sun god. Having a halo behind the saints, and even monarchs, was not to depict holiness but to celebrate that glow of the sun (Davis, p. 75). This can be seen in Constantine's coins before embracing Christianity as part of his allegiance to the sun god. This halo can also be seen in pictures of Hindu gods. A similar symbol is sometimes seen in the middle of a cross to show a sunburst in honor of the sun god. I find it interesting that Constantine's vision included a halo.

Cathedrals and Chapels. Samuel Boyd (2020) has published research on the origins of these essential church structures. While Christians often worshiped in various homes or sheltered in the catacombs during persecution, it wasn't until Constantine that these structures were produced. Many of these churches or cathedrals were previously pagan temples. They also became associated with imperial leadership:

> "The second major source for early Christian churches was Roman administrative buildings. The very name cathedral means "seat" and in Roman society referred to the location where governors would adjudicate and oversee their districts. When the pope speaks from his seat of power, he speaks "ex-cathedra.""

While Cathedrals were often impressive, chapels were smaller structures for worship. These structures often housed artifacts of spiritual significance. The name 'chapel' is associated with a story of a cloak worn by Jesus and placed in a place of worship for ordinary people to see.

> "These small structures were known as chapels, derived from the Latin Capella for "little cloak." These spaces of worship did not have musical instruments to accompany the service. As a result, the word 'a Capella,' meaning "according to the chapel" or "in the chapel style," reflects the manner of worship in the small church. (Boyd, 2020)."

Church Steeples. Each of the previous examples has been associated with pagan symbols. This is also true of the traditional church steeple. The shape of the steeple is in the form of an obelisk. These structures in I Kings 17: 9-11 are called Asherim, on every hill or under a green tree.

> "While the Church considers them a staple in architecture, they are deeply rooted in the Pagan worship of the sun god Ra. They are found on almost every continent in the world and were around long before the Church started using them. These are officially called Obelisks. They were constructed as a sort of memorial or statement by the Pagans in their worship of Ra. It is representative of fertility as it resembles the male reproductive organ, which is forever "fertile" (Church Steeples, Biblical Truth)."

Christmas. Most people think that the exact time of the birth of Christ is not known. There has been much speculation as to the approximate date. However, there seemed to be a consensus between Constantine and the early Christians. To attract pagans to this holiday, it was decided to use the winter solstice as the time of celebration.

> "December 25th was when the Old Roman Empire celebrated the birth of the sun god Sol Invictus,

> (Constantine's god). This was [already] a major holiday in Greece and Rome. All the sun gods from all countries, Horus, Osiris, Hercules, Adonis, Bacchus, Jupiter, and Tammuz, among others, were said to be born on this day. All evolved from the Babylonian religion (Davis, p. 88)."

There are many pagan symbols attached to this holiday – too many to enumerate. The puritans in the US officially banned the celebration of Christmas. Notice the theme of sun gods and the growth of Christian traditions. It was not commonly celebrated in the US until after 1776 (Controversies of Christmas, Wikipedia).

Easter. This holiday is particularly interesting. The date is straightforward since it is associated with the lunar calendar and the Jewish Passover. However, it is named after a pagan goddess (Oester), and the traditions associated with it are not Christian. Some point to fertility practices, such as celebrating eggs and bunnies. Even a bunny giving out baskets with chocolates and treats is rather odd. These traditions have nothing to do with the resurrection of Jesus (Weston, Easter, the Untold Story). Some say Christians used the pagan holiday to introduce pagans to the risen Christ.

Even the sunrise service has pagan origins in the celebration of Oester's partnership and reverence of the Canaanite sun god Tammuz:

> "…describing a "sunrise service," as the sun rises from the east [from which the sun rises]. Such practices go back for thousands of years, linking the sun with ancient pagan deities. As historian Alexander Hislop observed, "Long before the fourth century, and long before the Christian era itself, a festival was celebrated among the heathen, at that precise time of the year, in honour of the birth of the son of the Babylonian queen of heaven; and it may fairly be presumed that, in order to conciliate the heathen, and to swell the number of the nominal adherents of Christianity, the same festival was adopted by the Roman Church, giving it only the name of Christ. This tendency on the part of Christians to meet

> Paganism halfway was very early developed" (*The Two Babylons*, pp. 93). Festivals focusing on the solstice days were observed in the name of pagan gods long before there was any "Christian" idea of celebrating Christmas or Easter (Weston)!"

Why does any of this matter? The early Christians were careful not to mingle their practices or beliefs with the surrounding pagan culture. With the advent of Constantine, we see no hesitation in mixing our faith with pagan customs. Before Constantine, lifestyle and faithfulness were paramount for Christians. It did not depend on externals. Christians were considered atheists because they had no external symbols or tokens of a physical religion. That all changed with Constantine. This would eventually culminate in statues of saints, icons, and visible tokens of faith.

Please don't misunderstand. I have no desire to remove your enjoyment of any of these things. I love Christmas and Easter. Let's not pretend it hasn't become a secular holiday. Cathedrals are beautiful! The cross can be an icon of comfort. Christmas should be fun and a time of celebration. Easter is a glorious time of year and a time to celebrate the resurrection of Christ. I only ask that you recognize that many of these religious and worldly attractions have non-Christian roots. Look deeper into your faith and spirituality and avoid being distracted by these superficial things.

Discussion:

1. Why do you think the early church so quickly embraced Constantine's vision of Christianity?
2. In what ways were the 'norms of Christ' changed to reflect the values of the Roman Empire?
3. Do you think that the pagan origins of some of our Christian traditions make any difference to our faith currently?
4. In what ways do you think that Easter and Christmas are still paganized? How are Christians affected?
5. How can some of these pagan elements of our faith become distractions to spiritual growth?

CHAPTER 6: THE CHRISTIANIZATION OF SOCIETY

Emperor Constantine profoundly impacted Christianity, whether you believe he had a conversion experience. Likewise, Christianity affected the entire Roman Empire and, eventually, the world. This phenomenon had never been seen before – the exceptional partnership of the sacred with the secular.

Why did the pagans of the Roman Empire capitulate so quickly and completely? Constantine favored Christianity from AD 312 but still allowed pagan and other forms of worship. It wasn't until the Edict of Thessalonica, issued on 27 February AD 380, that Christianity became the Roman Empire's official religion, with other forms of worship outlawed (Edict of Thessalonica, Wikipedia). This event codified the Nicene Creed as applicable to all Roman territories.

Paganism and the Roman Empire, had run their course and needed a spiritual revolution. Rome was coming to its inevitable end, and the Church would lead.

> …it is not difficult to see why the Church triumphed and why the nations acquiesced as readily as they did in the downfall of paganism. The reason is that the world had grown stale. It had outlived all its old ideals. It was sick of doubt, weary of bloodshed and strife, and nervously apprehensive, we can hardly question, of the cataclysm that was to burst upon the West and submerge it before another century was over. The philosophies were worn out. The gods themselves had grown grey. There was a general atmosphere of numbness and decrepitude. Men wanted consolation and hope. Christianity

> alone could supply it, and though Christianity itself had lost its early joyousness, freshness, and simplicity, it retained unimpaired its marvelous powers to console. To a world tired of questioning and search it returned an answer for which it claimed the sanction of absolute Truth… Nevertheless, few can seriously doubt that the triumph of the Christian Church was an unspeakable boon to mankind. The Roman Empire was doomed. Its downfall was certain and, on the whole, was even to be desired, so long as its civilisation was not wholly wiped out and the genius of past generations was not wholly destroyed (Firth, pp. 163-165)."

The essence of the Christian faith is the comfort that Jesus provides. He identified with the poor and powerless. He loved and (loves) unconditionally. This was a remarkable aspect of this new religion. You didn't need to be born into a place of privilege. You could accept this gift and enjoy a promise of eternal life. He comforts us while suffering and brings us into a new family for physical and spiritual support.

Christianity was incorporated into the rule of many nations. While there were also many wars and hideous events throughout history, we can say that, for the ordinary person, the faith found in Christ was comforting. Unfortunately, leaders of the Church and the State used this newfound faith to manipulate the masses. For hundreds of years, men would be sent on the Crusades, thinking they were honoring God in slaughtering men, women, and children.

Having such power and authority based on the combined legitimacy of government and religion was bound to produce exploitation of power. To link the throne's influence with the realm of heaven and hell, there would be abuse and victimization. It's easy to justify cruelty to one's enemies when we can also see them as God's enemies. The

Old Testament seems to justify this approach. Constantine continued in this same framework when he used his mystical sign of the cross to destroy his enemies on the battlefield.

> "Beginning at least with Constantine's conversion, the followers of the Crucified have perpetrated gruesome acts of violence under the sign of the cross. Over the centuries, the seasons of Lent and Holy Week were, for the Jews, times of fear and trepidation. Muslims also associate the cross with violence; crusaders' rampages were undertaken under the sign of the cross (Volv, Miroslav, 2008, p.5)."

There is no doubt that much carnage and destruction have resulted from a severe form of Christianity. Yet, much good has been produced by adherents of the faith. These faithful practitioners have demonstrated a sacrificial love that is remarkable. Many missionaries, such as Mother Teresa, and many martyrs of the faith, stood up to religious and political regimes, such as Martin Luther King, Jr, and Billy Graham (to name a few). Besides the famous, a vast number of individuals have helped the poor without any desire for recognition or profit.

The Gospel of Christ has been preached through the power of the Holy Spirit, and hearts have responded. Despite those in authority abusing their positions, we see many who have been called to a life of love, humility, and service. Unfortunately, some leaders still take advantage of their position of authority and manipulate or injure the vulnerable. We still use the Bible as a weapon. I have met many who have been injured physically, mentally, or spiritually by misguided Christians or those in positions of authority.

What can be done to unleash the power of the Gospel and release it from the framework of position, power, and pride?

Discussion:

1. Why do you think the pagan gods failed the people of the Roman Empire while this new faith was embraced?
2. Do you know someone who was injured through the Christian faith? How?
3. In contrast, who has been a hero of the faith in your life?
4. Why do you think there has been so much damage done in the name of God in our society?
5. How can we help others understand the love of Christ?

CHAPTER 7: A FAITH CONSTRAINED

Once the Christian faith was legitimized, it might be imagined that our faith would have incredible freedom of expression. After all, there was astonishing access to scriptures and theological writings during the first 300 apostolic years. Access to the Bible was dramatically reduced for Christians after Constantine's reign. The Council of Nicaea was called by Emperor Constantine and met in AD 325 to establish a unified Church and doctrine. All other 'scriptures' were banned. Various churches and officials had adopted different texts and gospels that were not approved. That's why the Council of Hippo sanctioned only 27 books for the New Testament in AD 393.

Four years later, the Council of Cartage confirmed the same 27 books as authoritative New Testament books (Star, 2013). With the efforts to certify scripture, it is strange that the Church did not allow the laity access to these same scriptures for over 1,000 years. Professor Star provides documentation of the various edicts that prevented the laity from owning or even reading scripture in their language:

- Decree of the Council of Toulouse (AD 1229): "We prohibit also that the laity should be permitted to have the books of the Old or New Testament, but we most strictly forbid their having any translation of these books."
- Ruling of the Council of Tarragona of AD 1234: "No one may possess the books of the Old and New Testaments in the Romance language, and if anyone possesses them he must turn them over to the local bishop within eight days after the promulgation of this decree, so that they may be burned..."
- Proclamations at the Ecumenical Council of Constance in AD 1415: Oxford professor, and theologian John Wycliffe, was the first (AD 1380) to translate the New Testament into English

to "...helpeth Christian men to study the Gospel in that tongue in which they know best Christ's sentence." For this "heresy" Wycliffe was posthumously condemned by Arundel, the archbishop of Canterbury. By the Council's decree, "Wycliffe's bones were exhumed and publicly burned and the ashes were thrown into the Swift River."

- The fate of William Tyndale in AD 1536: William Tyndale was burned at the stake for translating the Bible into English. According to Tyndale, the Church forbid owning or reading the Bible to control and restrict the teachings and to enhance their power and importance.

If it was so important to have agreement on the contents of the Christian Bible, why was it forbidden to be read by the populace? Why prevent the Bible from being written in the languages of the people? The writings of the apostles were powerful and transforming. The ordinary person relied on hearing the scriptures expounded upon by the clergy. How could they check to see if what was being said was true? They couldn't. This made it easy to manipulate them. It was also during the Crusades that the Emperors and Kings could fuel hatred of the unbeliever through the vitriolic preaching of the clergy.

Now almost every household has access to the Bible (in numerous translations) in their home or via online resources. Why, then, are we still failing in our spiritual growth? Despite having access to scripture, many are not growing in their relationship with the living Savior. We still seem plagued by doctrinal arrogance, egocentric thinking, and dualistic behavior.

Discussion:

1. Imagine you did not have access to the Bible but depended on official clergy to understand God's Word. What would happen to your faith?
2. Paul commended the Bereans (Acts 17: 10-15) because they studied their Bible to see if Paul was correct in his application. Even the most authoritative preachers need to be checked. Why is this important?

3. There are several possible reasons why scripture was not provided to lay people. What are some that come to mind?
4. Can full access to the Bible cause problems controlling spiritual understanding and discussion within congregations?
5. In what ways do we take our privilege to access the Bible for granted?

CHAPTER 8: ALTERNATIVE TO A VIOLENT RELIGIOUS EMPIRE

I am so thankful that the Church continues bringing comfort and a relationship with Christ to many. However, there are problems with how our faith is practiced. Even so, we still have the Constantine mentality of waging war and dominating others. We tend to be divisive, materialistic, argumentative, sectarian, political, prejudiced, and judgmental as a religion. There is no difference between being a Christian and a non-believer.

We are critical of other faiths, denominations, and cultures. We fail in the Christian basics of loving others. When strangers enter our churches, they often do not feel welcome. We consider our churches a club that only the privileged should join. We are organized by professional clergy who seek more numbers and often fail to minister to the needs of the poor and struggling. We separate Christians into the professional class and the laity.

Why are we struggling to bring relevance to our religion in a world that desperately needs the Spirit of Christ? Why is the Prince of Peace irrelevant to our culture? Perhaps it is because our faith is still weaponized as it was with Constantine. The Franciscan Monk, Richard Rohr (2022), has an interesting perspective on our failed religion as cited in one of his online devotionals entitled "Rebuilding from the Bottom Up":

> "Our religion is not working well: suffering, fear, violence, injustice, greed, and meaninglessness still abound. This is not even close to the reign of God that Jesus taught. And we must be frank: in their behavior and impact upon the world, Christians are not much different than other people…

> Let's be honest: religion has probably never had such a bad name. Christianity is now seen as "irrelevant" by some, "toxic" by many, and often as a large part of the problem rather than any kind of solution. Some of us are almost embarrassed to say we are Christian because of the negative images that the word conjures in others' minds. Young people especially are turned off by how judgmental, exclusionary, impractical, and ineffective Christian culture seems to be.
>
> Most Christians have not been taught *how* to plug into the "mind of Christ"; thus, they often reflect the common mind of power, greed, and violence instead. The dualistic mind reads reality in simple binaries—good and bad, right and wrong—and thinks itself smart because it chooses one side. This is getting us nowhere."

Our problem is that we continue to embrace the same things Emperor Constantine did: power, prestige, privilege, and prosperity. This is getting us nowhere. We desire bigger congregations, more attractive edifices, large ministerial budgets, high-income worshippers, well-paid clergy, perfectly explained doctrine, talented young musicians, entertaining youth programs, impressive religious performances – and phony, insincere smiles. Many are leaving mainline churches and are non-affiliated with any denomination (called 'none'). We must stop running our churches on the business model where the pastor is the CEO. What can we do to change this?

We need to approach our practice of faith with a more sincere and open response to Jesus' call for us to make disciples. I worship in an urban outreach of a mainline church that ministers to the homeless, alcoholics, people in recovery, and those on the edge of society. I consider myself one of them. We meet at about ten small round tables with 6-8 people around them to discuss a Bible passage. There is no sermon. In the end, representatives from several tables tell us what they discussed. There are some mature believers in this group. Each week we are blessed with incredible wisdom and valuable insights. Why is this so surprising? Why are we so arrogant? Why do we want to fit people into neat categories? Again, Richard Rohr (2008) has an observation:

> "When we lead off with our judgments, love will seldom happen. Religion is almost always corrupted when the mind, which needs to make moral judgments about everything, is the master instead of the servant.
>
> Some would think that is the whole meaning of Christianity: to decide who's going to heaven and who isn't, who is holy and unholy. This is much more a search for control than it is a search for truth, love, or God. It has to do with ego, which needs to pigeonhole everything to give itself that sense of "I know" and "I am in control…."
>
> When we are allowed to name certain individuals as "bad," persecution, scapegoating, and violence almost always follow. When we too easily presume that we are one of the "good" people, we largely live in illusion and prejudice. I say this as a religious person, but religion has been the justification of much of the violence in human history. God wanted to undercut that very violence at the beginning." (pp. 36-38)

An example for me was a young African American man who happened to sit at our table. I was impressed with his knowledge of the Bible and his insights into its application. I had not seen him before and asked how he knew so much of the Bible. I thought maybe he had been to Bible school or seminary. He explained that he learned about the Bible in prison and had just gotten released. I was blessed and humbled.

This is only part of our approach to discipleship. We also provide tools for spiritual growth. The goal is not to indoctrinate but to introductions to faith and healing. We encourage small study groups, accountability groups, group meditation, Bible study, online messages, and open discussions. The key is genuine and authentic interpersonal connection.

Here is our Community Statement for the Portico's downtown campus. I wonder how many churches would embrace this statement. We read this out loud before every Sunday meeting to remind us about our mission.

> "Our church community is diverse. It includes people from different backgrounds and faith traditions. There are folks in recovery, those who might need recovery, others struggling with faith, new and long-time followers of Jesus, agnostics, skeptics, and people exploring the idea of a higher power. Many are seeking a spiritual connection in a non-traditional setting, or have been dissatisfied with, or burned in the past by a church.
>
> We agree not to make assumptions about others and challenge ourselves to be open and sensitive. We don't assume fluency in the Bible and do our best to explain churchy jargon and language.
>
> We gather to build relationships in this Sunday gathering through conversation, contemplative practice, and authenticity. We gather in groups throughout the week and intentionally serve the city and world in ways that address equality, housing insecurity, and economic challenge.
>
> We do all of this because we have come to find that the message of Jesus is not for Christianity, but for humanity. And as such, we strive together to Make God's Love Real to others through Conversation, Connection, and Community Change." https://theportico.org/spiritual-community/

Notice how this statement acknowledges that we are all at different stages of growth. It can be intimidating going into a church not knowing what is expected of you. This fellowship allows everyone to be authentic and no one to pretend to have all the answers. This open meeting on Sunday becomes an entry into a conversation and relationship.

How can we become more of what Jesus expects of his followers? Perhaps this could be a start:

1. Stop running the church as a business or a club
2. Sacrificially love others as Christ loved us
3. Don't tell people what to think; help them explore their doubts; avoid indoctrination
4. Encourage everyone to see God in all
5. Provide tools and opportunities to embrace a relationship with Jesus
6. Don't preach at congregations; have face-to-face conversations with people
7. Avoid telling others what to believe; show them how to believe and live
8. Always listen and make sure you understand before you talk
9. Avoid political or divisive talk which creates barriers; build bridges
10. Encourage unity through love and understanding, even with those with whom we disagree

I am sure that this sounds very strange. Where is the liturgy? What's wrong with preaching doctrine? Why not do church the way it has always been done? It always worked for us! But did it? You might say we need big churches and intellectual theologians. We need to have a faith that is contemporary, attractive, and youthful. Perhaps this is the time for change and the removal of Constantine's imprint. Here is what Brian McLaren says:

> "For centuries, Christianity has presented itself as an "organized religion"—a change-averse institution . . . that protects and promotes a timeless system of beliefs that were handed down fully formed in the past. Yet Christianity's actual history is a story of change and adaptation. We Christians

> have repeatedly adapted our message, methods, and mission to the contours of our time. What might happen if we understand the core Christian ethos as creative, constructive, and forward-leaning—as an "organizing religion" that challenges all institutions (including its own) to learn, grow, and mature toward a deepening, enduring vision of reconciliation with God, self, neighbor, enemy, and creation?" (McLaren, 2016, p. 3).

Of course, Constantine would disagree with all of this. He wouldn't understand how you could build a religion based on love, gentleness, and generosity. How could that create an atmosphere of control? He would insist that we use power or position. That religious experiment was done, and it failed. The time for a battlefield religion is over. Not only can we be the salt of the earth and the light of the world with love, but I believe it's the only way Jesus would have it!

Discussion:

1. What surprised you as you read the Portico's Community Statement? Why?
2. Do you think the church sometimes has a business or country club approach to ministry? How is that not helpful?
3. Do we tend to have a 'battlefield' mentality about our religion? How is that expressed?
4. What can we do to encourage others to have a relationship with Jesus?
5. What's the difference between telling someone what to believe and showing them how to believe?

St. Louis Cathedral in New Orleans. Elegant pews with the main focus on the altar and priest.

Portico Table Talk. People from all walks of life sit around tables and discuss a Bible passage.

Post Table Talk Panel. Volunteers share what was discussed about the Bible passage. No authorities – just people from the community.

EPILOGUE

Based on the problems with our organized religion, what should we do? Should we abandon a flawed religion as many are doing and be 'unchurched'? Perhaps start a new denomination? Maybe deconstruct Constantine's Christian religion and bring it back to a truly Christ-centered faith? None of these options are helpful. We must realize that while the church might be broken Jesus and His teachings are amazingly relevant and necessary for a time like ours.

The foundation of our organized religion is crumbling beneath our feet. Metaphorically, its 'residents' are running for the exits. It has failed to reflect the principles of Jesus. Organizationally it has been victorious over many peoples and nations for centuries. It was used by Constantine and those who followed him to wield position, power, control, and intellectual conformity. I am sickened by this model of Christianity. Our brand of Western religion is superficial, arrogant, paternalistic, and materialistic. How unlike the message that Jesus preached. Adherents to our faith do not represent Christ very well. It is hard to tell the difference between Christians and non-Christians. People of other faiths seem to display more of Christ's qualities than we who are members of His religion.

I suggest small accountability groups within every place of worship. Studying this book in a small group is a start. The dialogue must continue. Accountability and responsiveness to the Spirit must be encouraged. We must inspire each other to live authentic lives of faith and love. We are to throw off the "old man" and put on the "new man," as the Apostle Paul tells us:

> "But this is not the way you came to know Christ. Surely you heard of Him and were taught in Him—in keeping with the truth that is in Jesus—to put off

> your former way of life, your old self, which is being corrupted by its deceitful desires; to be renewed in the spirit of your minds; and to put on the new self, created to be like God in true righteousness and holiness. (Ephesians 4: 20-24)"

The Church needs reformation. For this to happen it is imperative that individual believers have a renewal of their faith. We have become so comfortable with the Christian 'organization' that we have forgotten about Jesus and His unique message of love and sacrifice. He doesn't want converts to a dogma; He desires disciples that follow Him and live out His teaching. We can make a difference within our faith by living it out humbly, lovingly, and authentically. I am not encouraging an exodus from our churches. Instead, I am encouraging an uprising of Christian leaders who see the Church as its people, not as assets, property, and numbers.

We continue to believe that all we need to unite the Church is the right doctrine and to communicate it effectively. We think that if everyone believed the same stuff, we would have to be united. That has been the denominational vision of Christianity. Just get the words right! We are using Constantine's strategy. Define what to believe and enforce the 'divide and conquer' mentality. This is the problem! We must stop thinking we need to have congregations believe the same phrases. Jesus has already brought unity through love. Here is what the Apostle Paul said:

> "As a prisoner for the Lord, then, I urge you to live a life worthy of the calling you have received. Be completely humble and gentle; be patient, bearing with one another in love. Make every effort to keep the unity of the Spirit through the bond of peace. There is one body and one Spirit, just as you were called to one hope when you were called; one Lord, one faith, one baptism; one God and Father of all, who is over all and through all and in all." (Ephesians 4: 1-6, NIV)

Constantine's approach brings competition, conflict, and contempt. Notice that Paul encourages us to "maintain" the unity of the

Spirit through peace, humility, patience, and love. This is not something that we have to create. It is already a reality that needs to be reinforced. Sadly, these concepts are lacking in our practice of faith. Please do not misunderstand, there are many churches where wonderful things happen. Unfortunately, too seldom is it reflected outside of the sanctuary. Here are the qualities that should distinguish us from those that are outside of the faith:

> "...serve one another humbly in love. For the entire law is fulfilled in keeping this one command: "Love your neighbor as yourself." If you bite and devour each other, watch out or you will be destroyed by each other."
>
> "So I say, walk by the Spirit, and you will not gratify the desires of the flesh. For the flesh desires what is contrary to the Spirit, and the Spirit what is contrary to the flesh. They are in conflict with each other, so that you are not to do whatever you want. But if you are led by the Spirit, you are not under the law..."
>
> "But the fruit of the Spirit is love, joy, peace, forbearance, kindness, goodness, faithfulness, gentleness and self-control. Against such things there is no law. Those who belong to Christ Jesus have crucified the flesh with its passions and desires. Since we live by the Spirit, let us keep in step with the Spirit. Let us not become conceited, provoking and envying each other." (Galatians 5: 13b-18; 22-24).

Here we see that Paul contrasts what will happen unless we walk by the Spirit, we will bite and devour each other. Without being led by God we are led by our own ego through conceit and are in constant conflict with each other. We become provocative and envious. This is the Constantine way! Instead, we should walk in the spirit which is the fruit of the Spirit. Whenever we meet or interact with others, we should always demonstrate these heavenly qualities.

Here is the prayer of Pastor Chan in his book entitled "Until Unity." I also pray that God will use this little book to stimulate discussion about how we should live out our faith in a way that dispels division and brings a real sense of unity to the Body of Christ. It is time for Constantine's Christian Empire to fall and for the Body of Christ to blossom forth in love and community.

> "My prayer in writing this book has been that we as a church could come to our senses and see all of the division and infighting as something contrary to God's design. I have been praying that God's people could recover the love and unity that the Bible consistently emphasizes. I have been asking God to create an army of people who believe we can be united in the love of Jesus through the empowerment of the Spirit." (Chan, 2021, p. 201)

Amen

Discussion:

1. Why not start a new denomination that goes back to the basic principles of Christianity?
2. What do you think is causing people to leave Christianity?
3. What aspects of Constantine's religious approach to faith disturb you?
4. How can you encourage spiritual growth within your own congregation?
5. Is it possible to live by the Spirit? How?
6. What are the next steps in your spiritual journey?

REFERENCES

Boyd, Samuel L. (2020). "What are the origins of Cathedrals and Chapels." https://theconversation.com/what-are-the-origins-of-cathedrals-and-chapels-143341 Accessed 24 November 2022.

Chan, Francis (2021). "Until Unity." David C Cook. Kindle Edition.

Christian History Institute. "#104: Tertullian's Defense" https://christianhistoryinstitute.org/study/module/tertullian. Accessed 9 November 2022.

Christmas Controversies. https://en.wikipedia.org/wiki/Christmas_controversies Accessed 24 November 2022.

Church Steeples. Biblical Truth. https://biblicaltruth.net/forbidden-things/obelisks-or-church-steeples/ Accessed 24 November 2022.

Constantine the Great. Wikipedia. https://en.wikipedia.org/wiki/Constantine_the_Great Accessed October 5, 2022.

Davis, Loren (2006). "The Paganization of Christianity." Chi Publishing: Tulsa, OK.

Denova, Rebecca (May 10, 2021). "Constantine's Conversion to Christianity." https://www.worldhistory.org/article/1737/constantines-conversion-to-christianity/ Accessed October 15, 2022.

Duchesne, Louis (2018). Early History of the Christian Church: From its Foundation to the End of the Fifth Century (Volume II). Florin Publishing. Kindle Edition.

Edict of Thessalonica. Wikipedia. https://en.wikipedia.org/wiki/Edict_of_Thessalonica Accessed November 25, 2022.

Firth, John B. (1904). "Constantine the Great: The Reorganization of the Empire and the Triumph of the Church." Making History. Kindle Edition

History, Hourly (2021). Constantine the Great: A Life from Beginning to End (Roman Emperors) Kindle Edition.

Jones, A.H.M. (2019). "Vision of Constantine before the battle of the Milvian Bridge." https://imperiumromanum.pl/en/article/vision-of-constantine-before-the-battle-of-the-milvian-bridge/ Accessed October 30, 2022.

Kee, Alistair (1982). "Constantine Versus Christ." Wiph and Stock Publishers: Eugene, OR.

McLaren, Brian D. (2016). "The Great Spiritual Migration: How the World's Largest Religion Is Seeking a Better Way to Be Christian" Convergent: New York.

Odahl, Charles Matson (2004). "Constantine and the Christian Empire" 2nd Ed. Routledge: NY.

Owles, R. Joseph. (2014). "The Didache: The Teaching of the Twelve Apostles." Kindle Edition.

Roberts, A and Donaldson, J. (Eds). (2014). "ANTE-NICENE FATHERS Volume 1 The Apostolic Fathers, Justin Martyr, Irenaeus, etc." Veritatis Splendor Publications. Kindle Edition.

Rohr, Richard (2008) "Things Hidden: Scripture as Spirituality." Franciscan Media, Cincinnati, OH

Rohr, Richard (May 22, 2022). "Rebuilding From the Bottom Up" https://cac.org/daily-meditations/redeeming-our-religion-2022-05-22/ Accessed 05/23/2022.

Star, Bernard (2013). Huffpost.com "Why Christians Were Denied Access to Their Bible for 1,000 Years." https://www.huffpost.com/entry/why-christians-were-denied-access-to-their-bible-for-1000-years_b_3303545 Accessed November 25, 2022

Tau. Wikipedia. https://en.wikipedia.org/wiki/Stauros Accessed 24 November 2022.

The Constantine Shift. Wikipedia. https://en.wikipedia.org/wiki/Constantinian_shift. Accessed October 5, 2022.

Volf, Miroslav (2008). "Christianity and Violence." In Hess, Richard S.; Martens, E.A. (eds.) War in the Bible and terrorism in the twenty-first century. Eisenbrauns Publishing: Winona Lake, IN.

Weston, Gerald E. "Easter: The Untold Story." https://www.tomorrowsworld.org/booklets/easter-the-untold-story?gclid=CjwKCAiAyfybBhBKEiwAgtB7fiEgI2V9IFfzG7ZA4mZGnJ6IW8QvHHlvoh_TJnQY_j3Ju63h4k5raRoCjEEQAvD_BwE Accessed 24 November 2022.

www.ingramcontent.com/pod-product-compliance
Lightning Source LLC
LaVergne TN
LVHW010121170826
845678LV00012B/2533

* 9 7 9 8 3 6 9 6 9 6 9 4 1 *